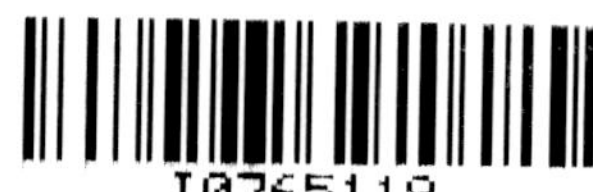

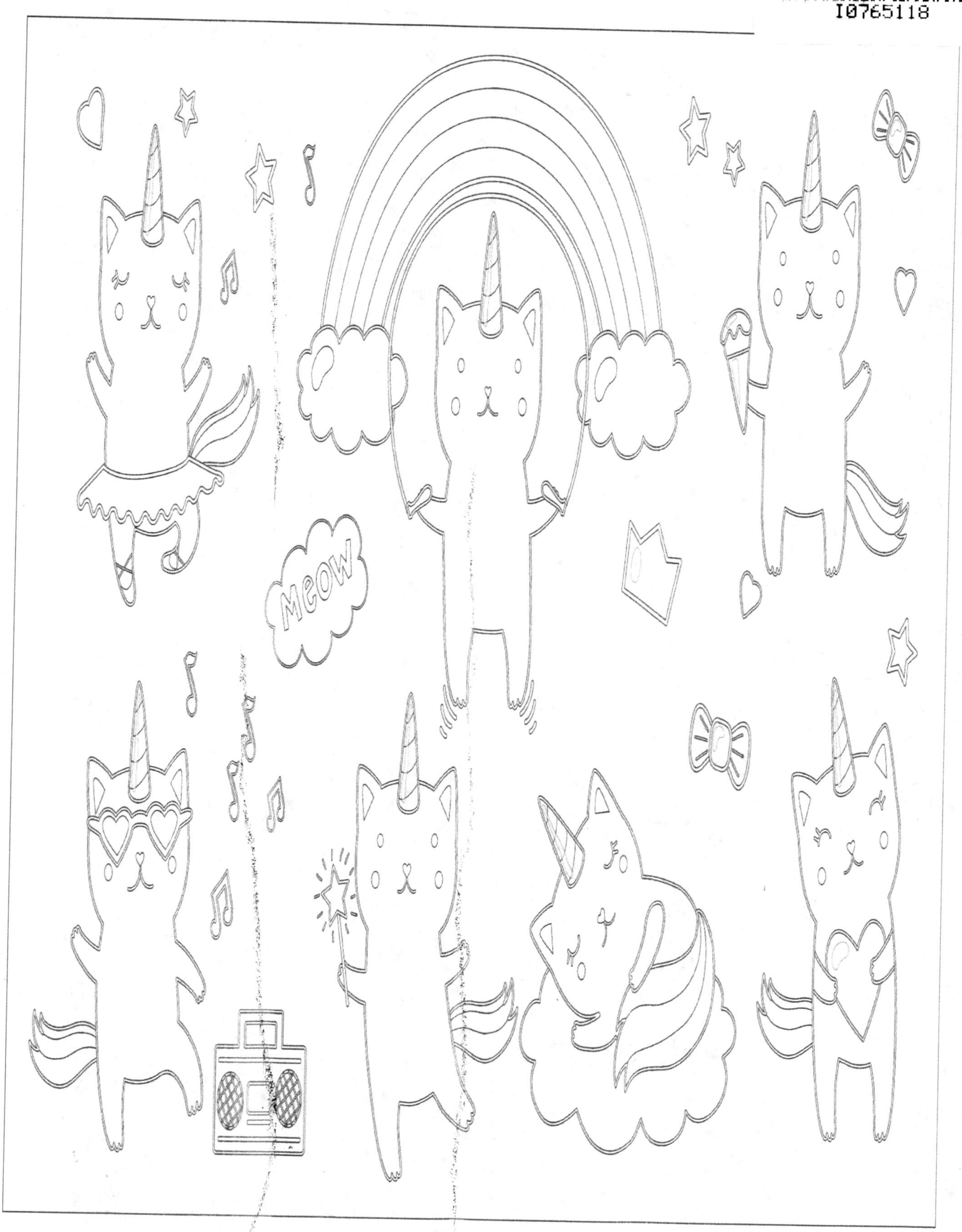

MeOW

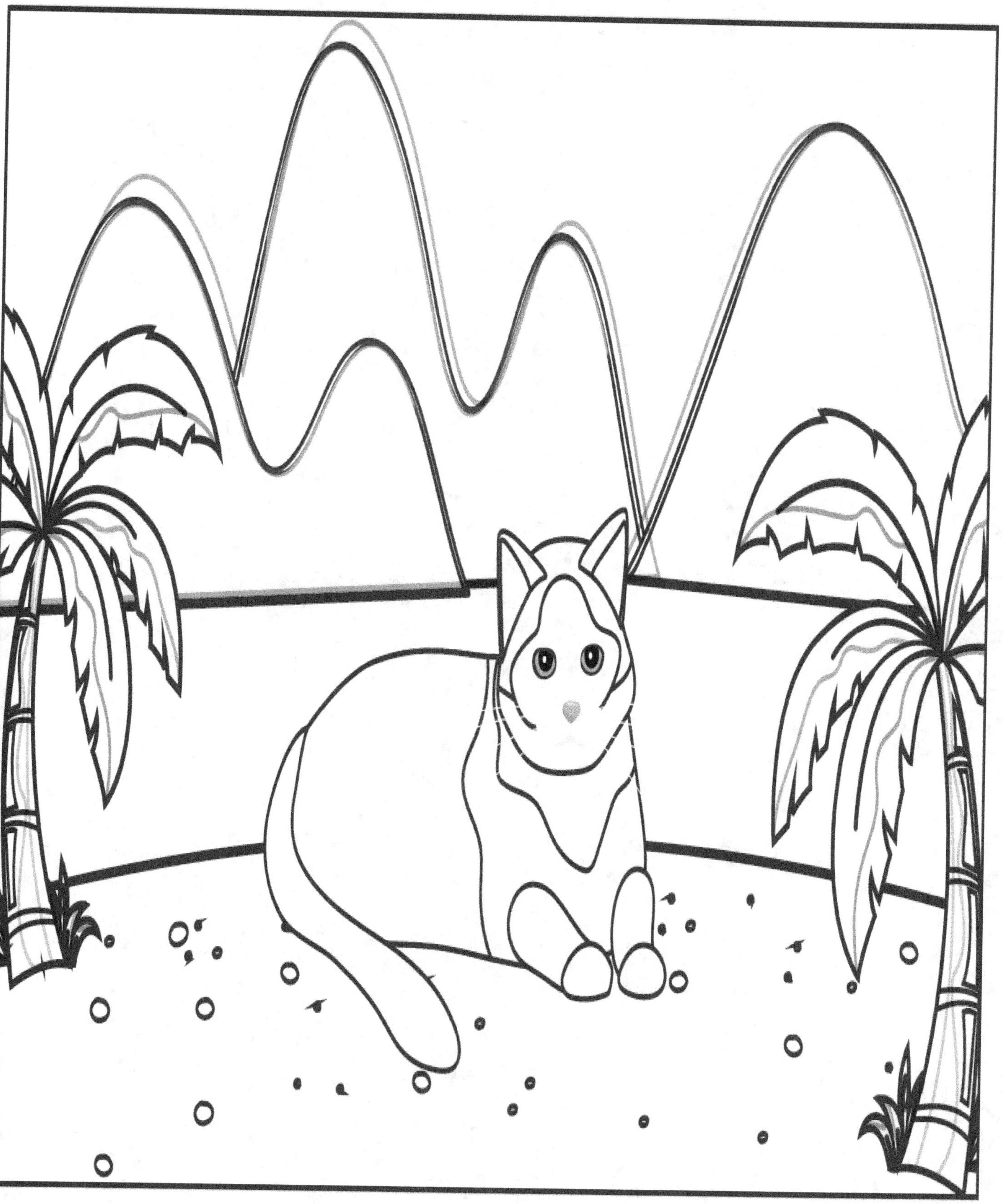

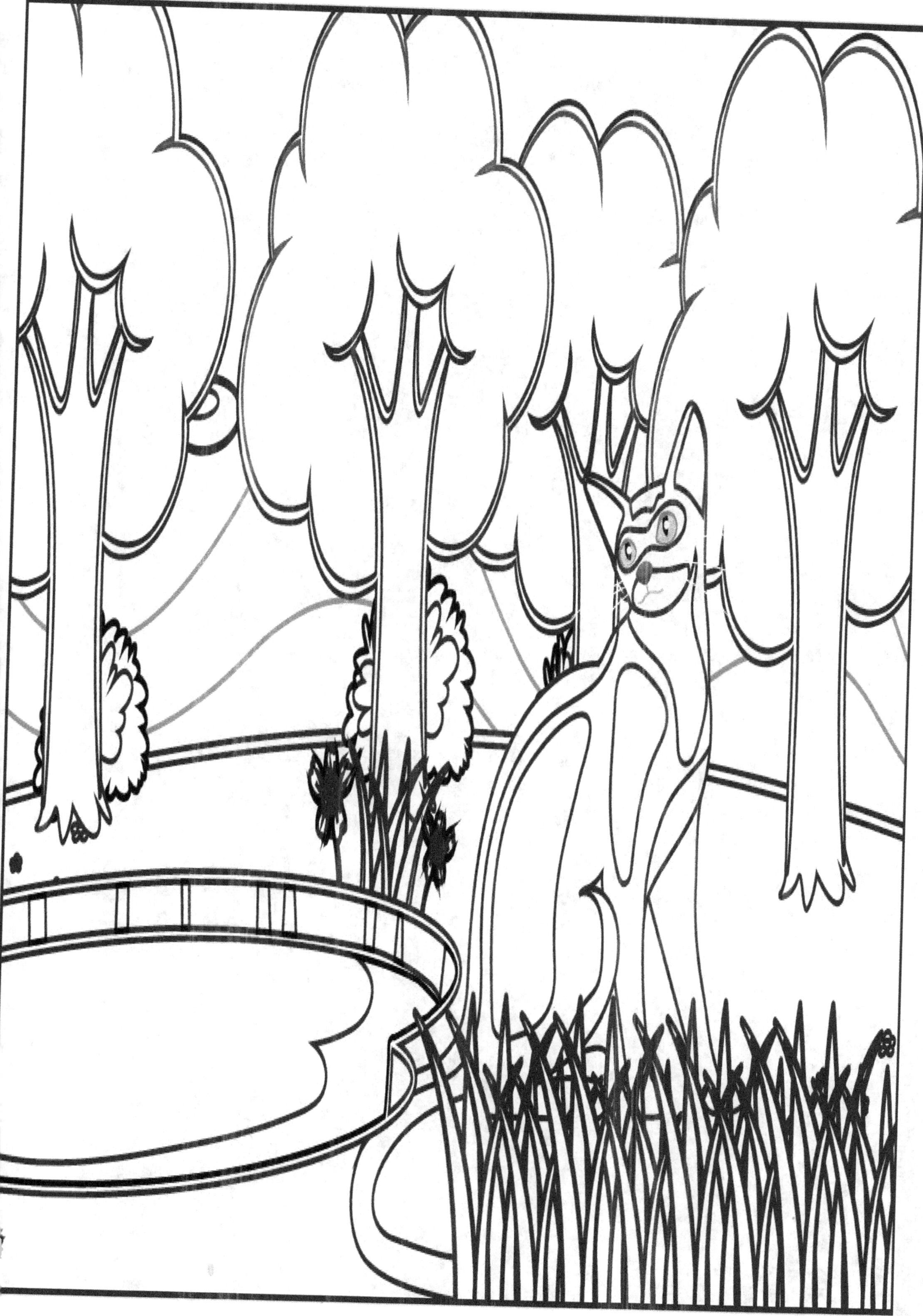

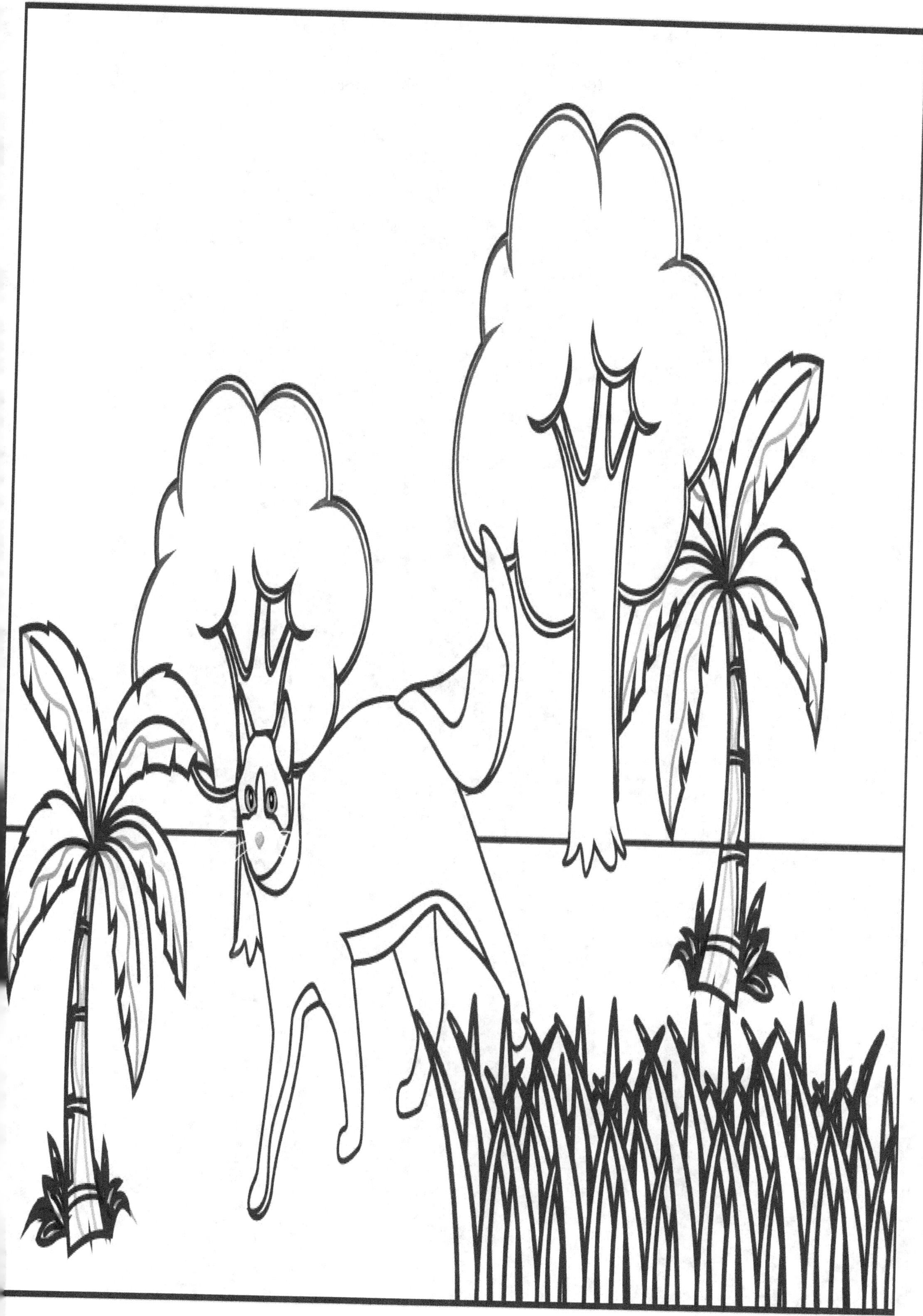

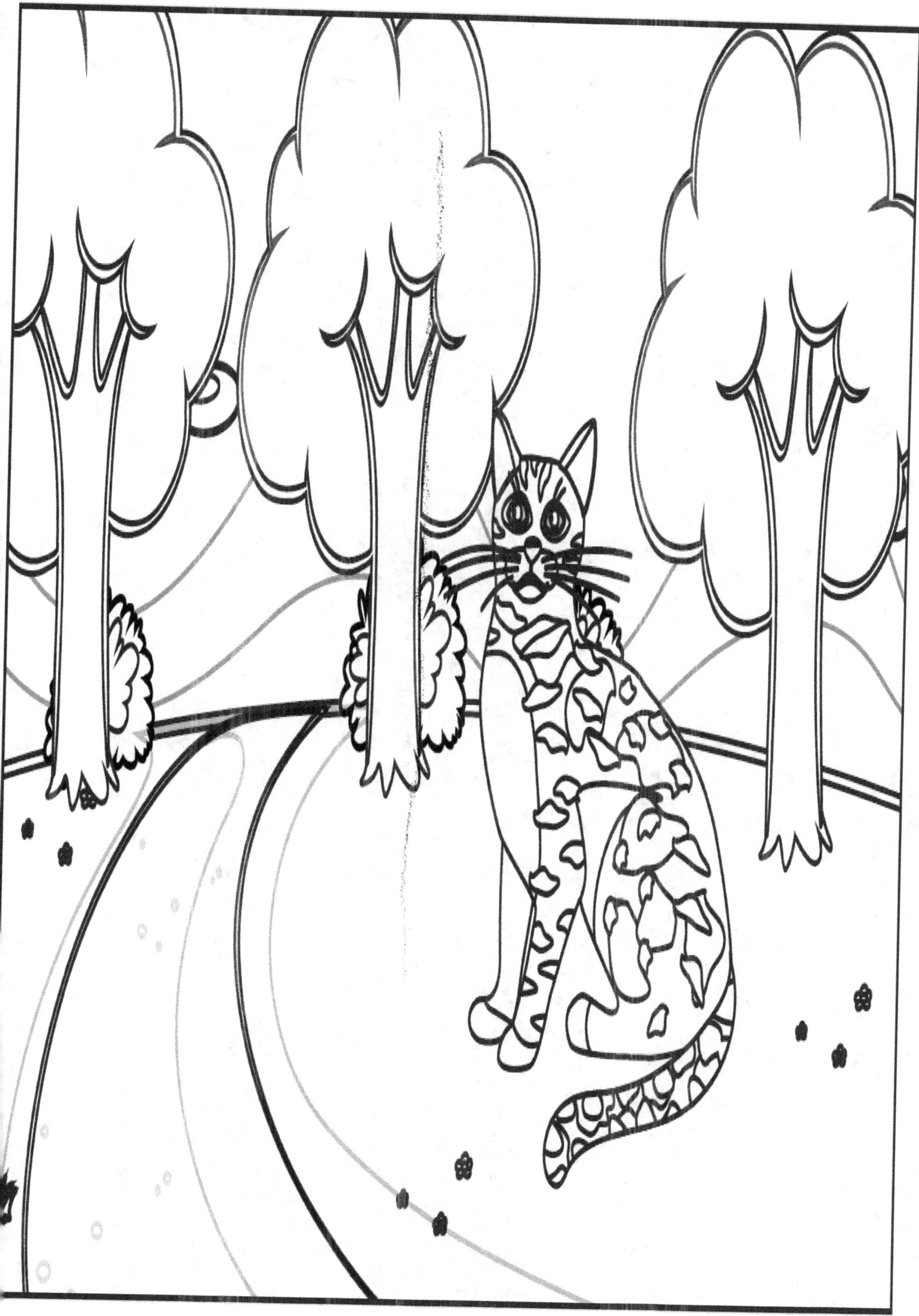

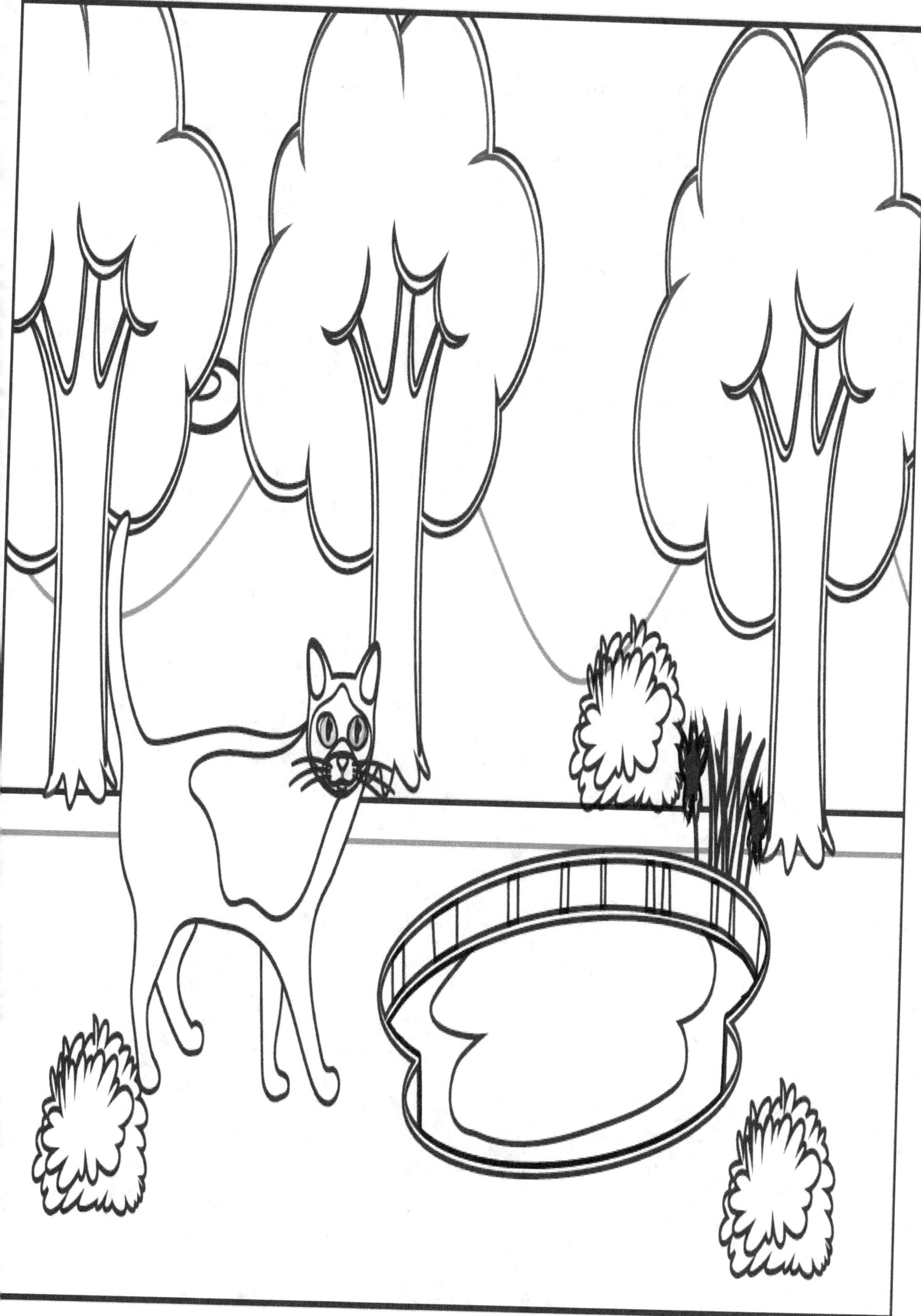

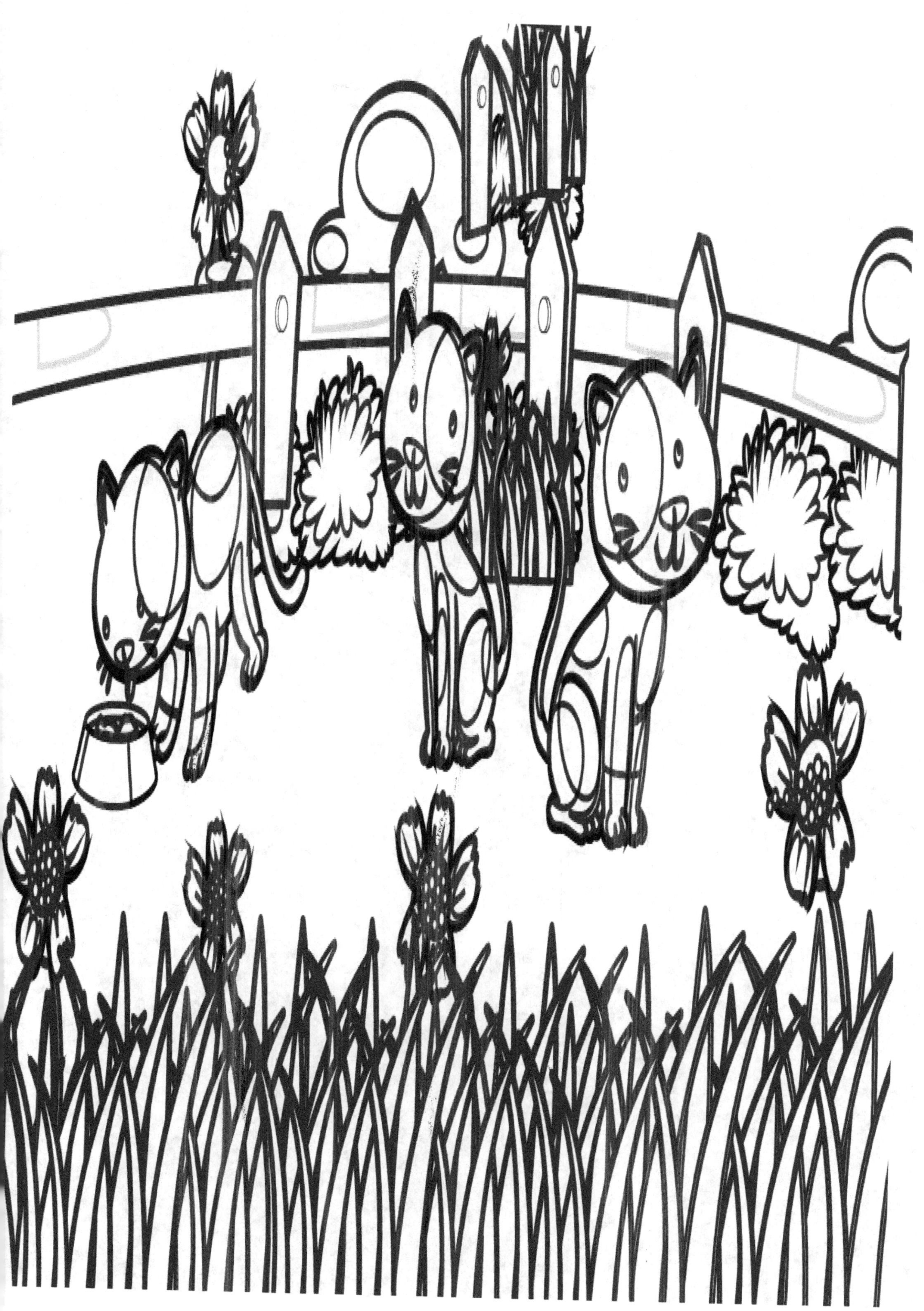

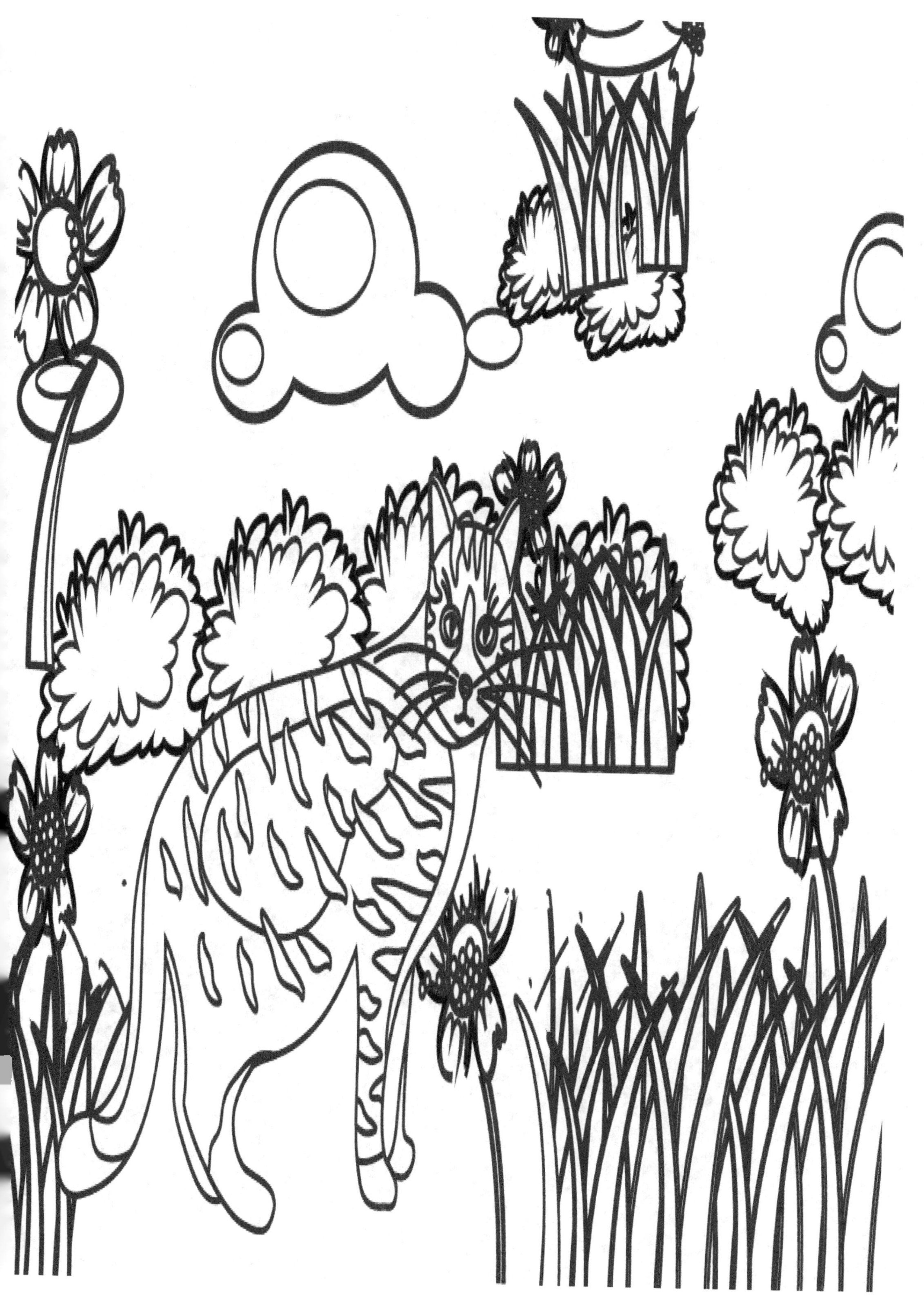

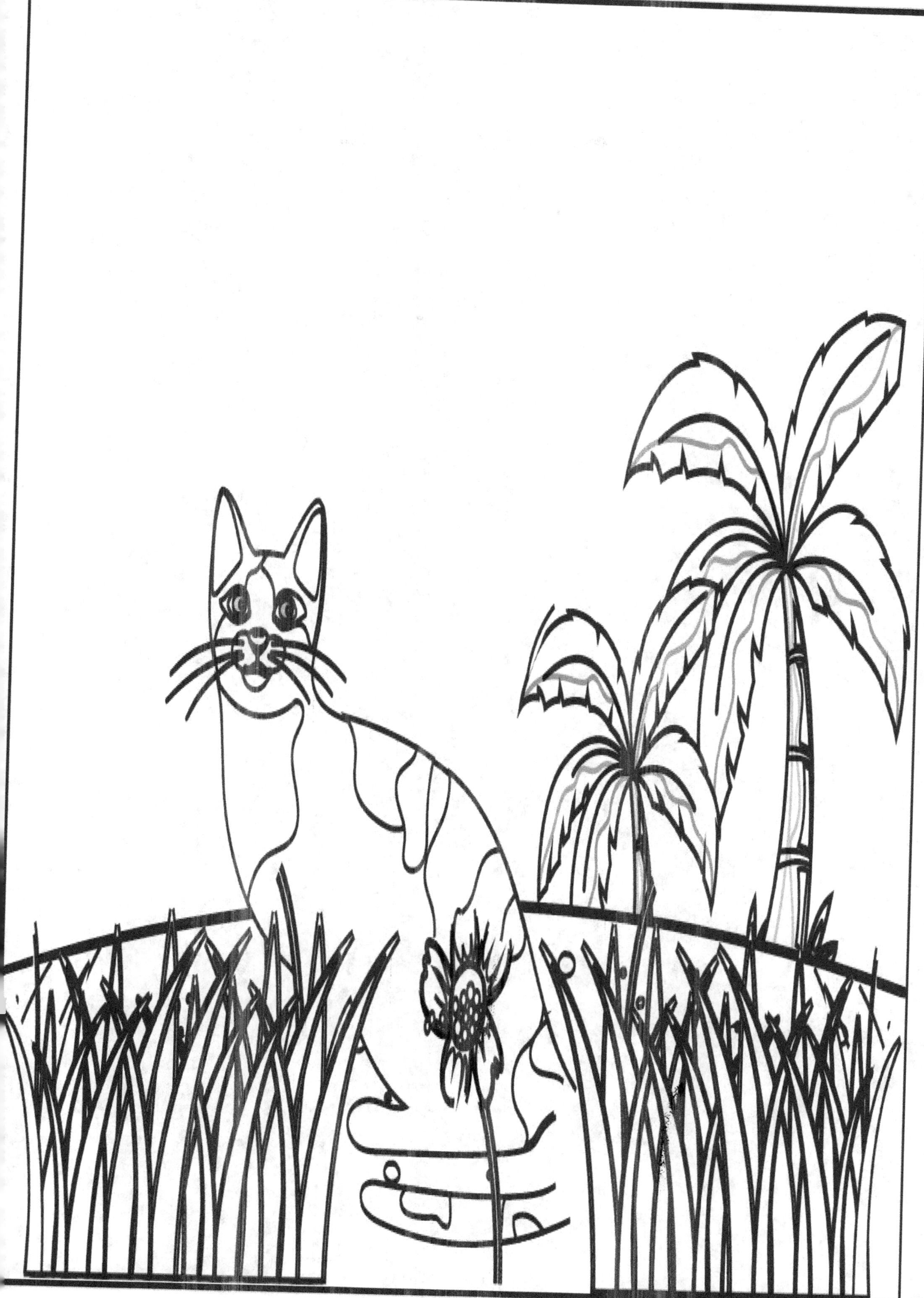

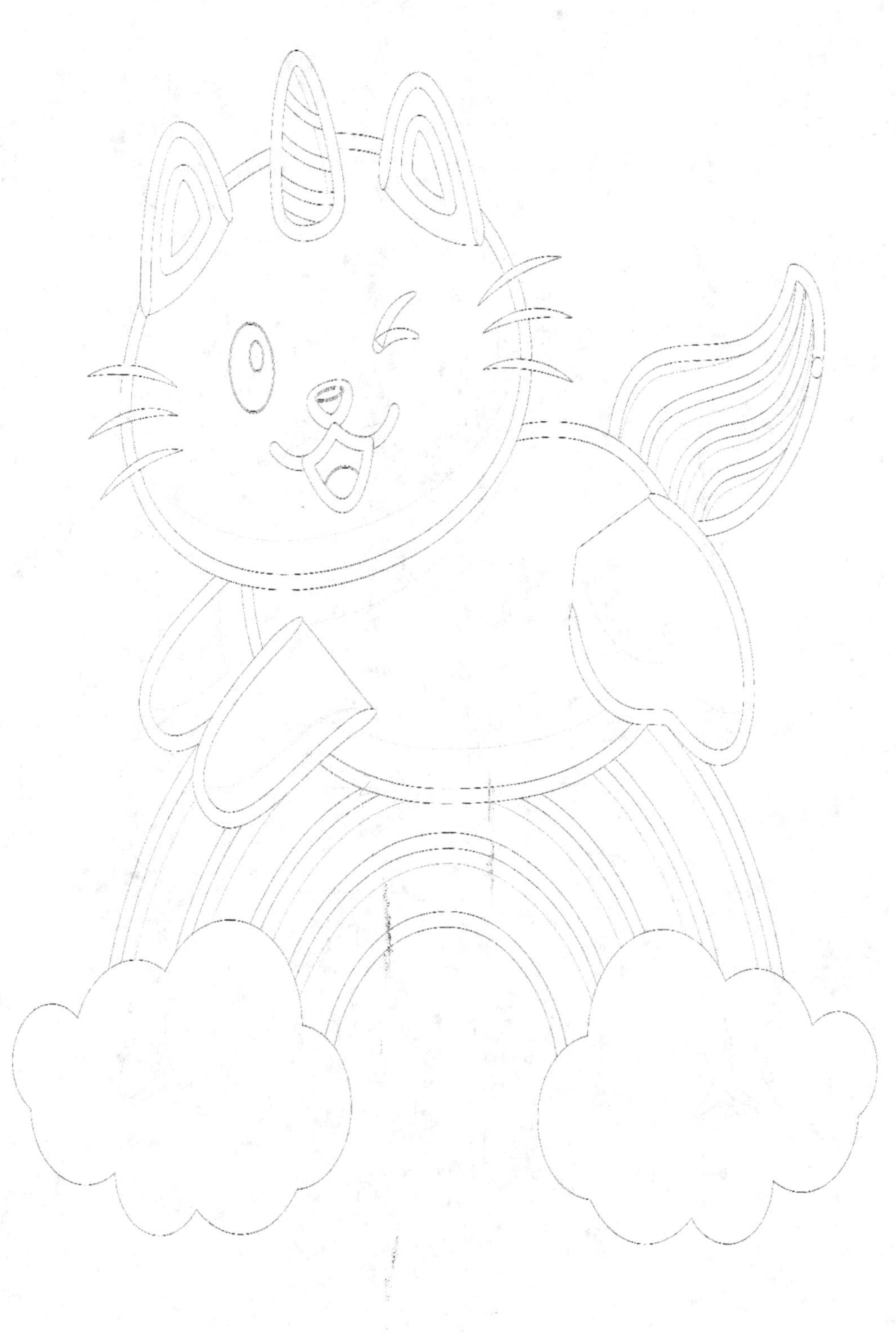

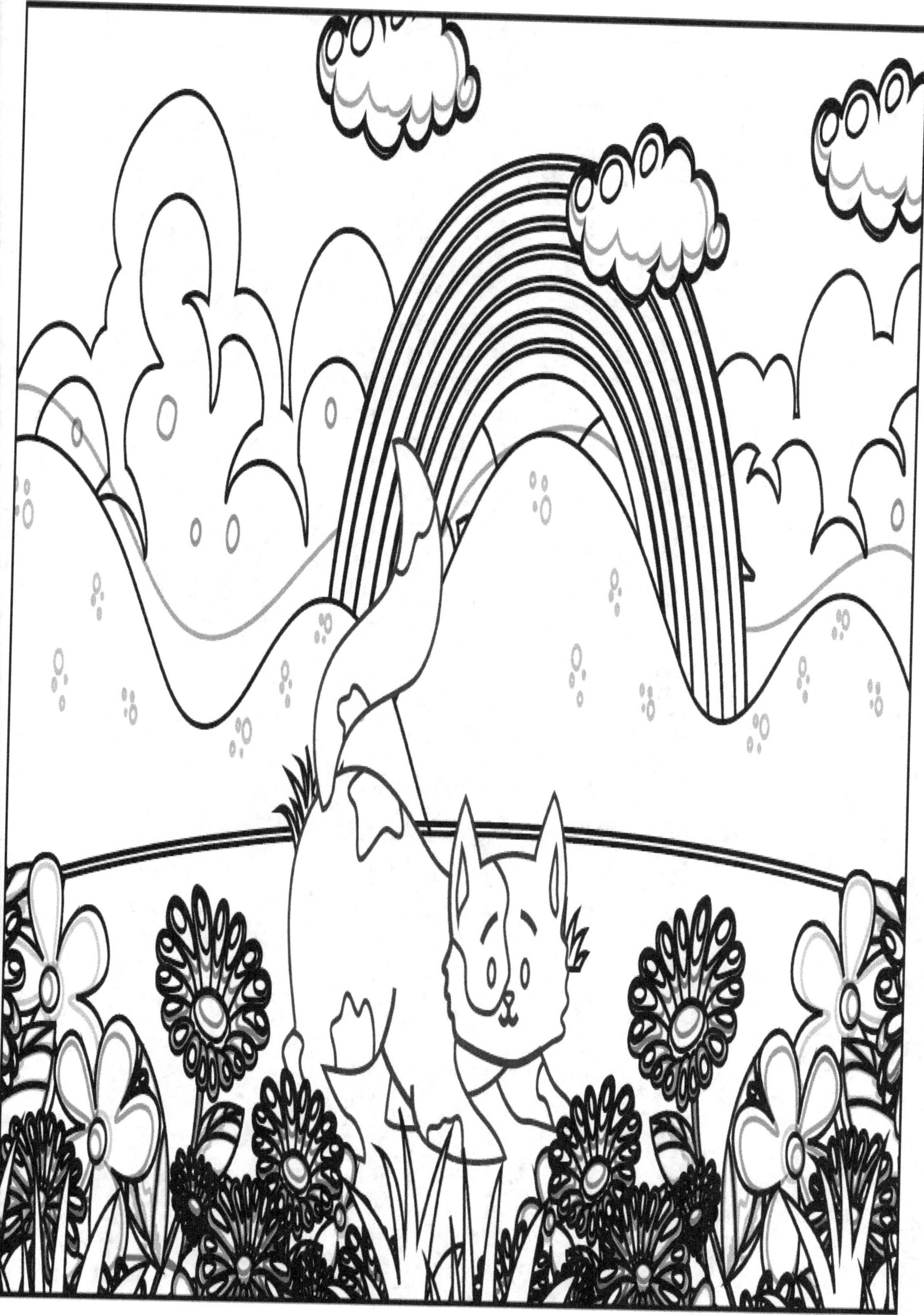

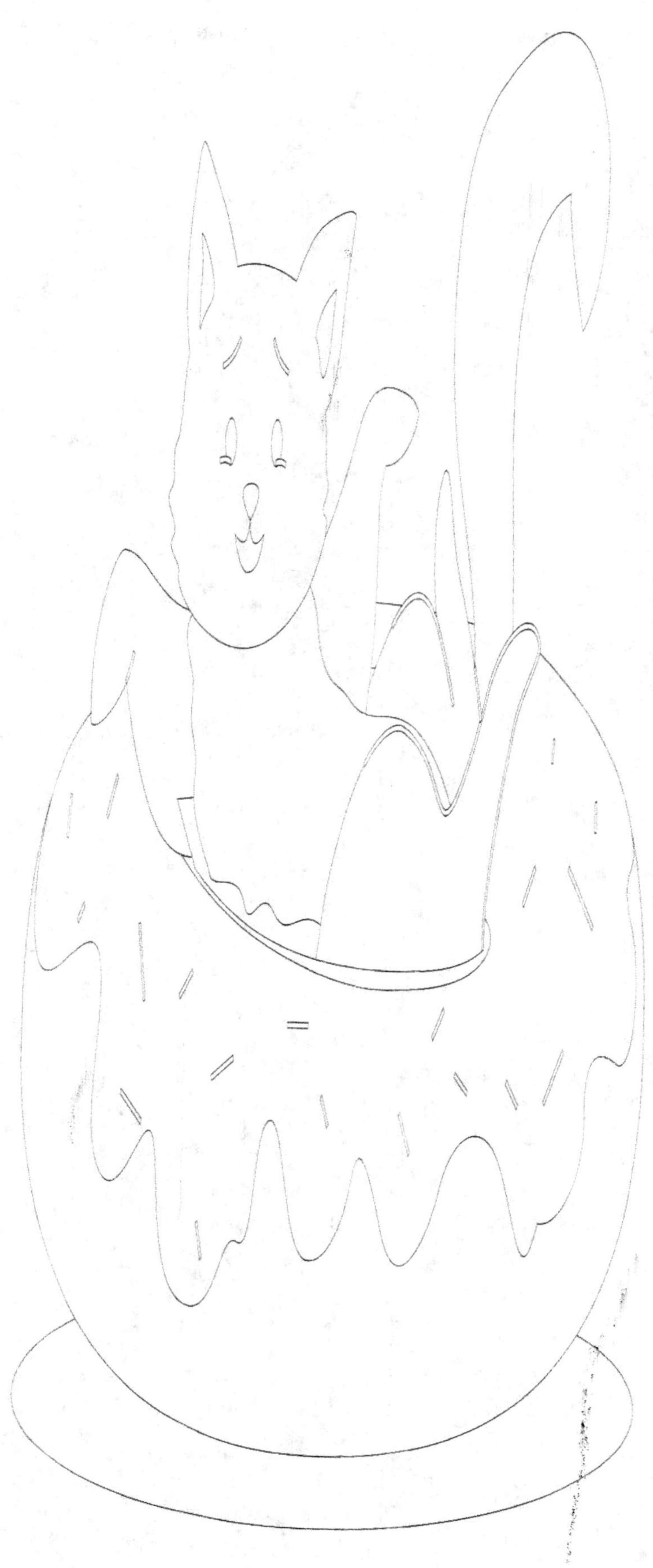

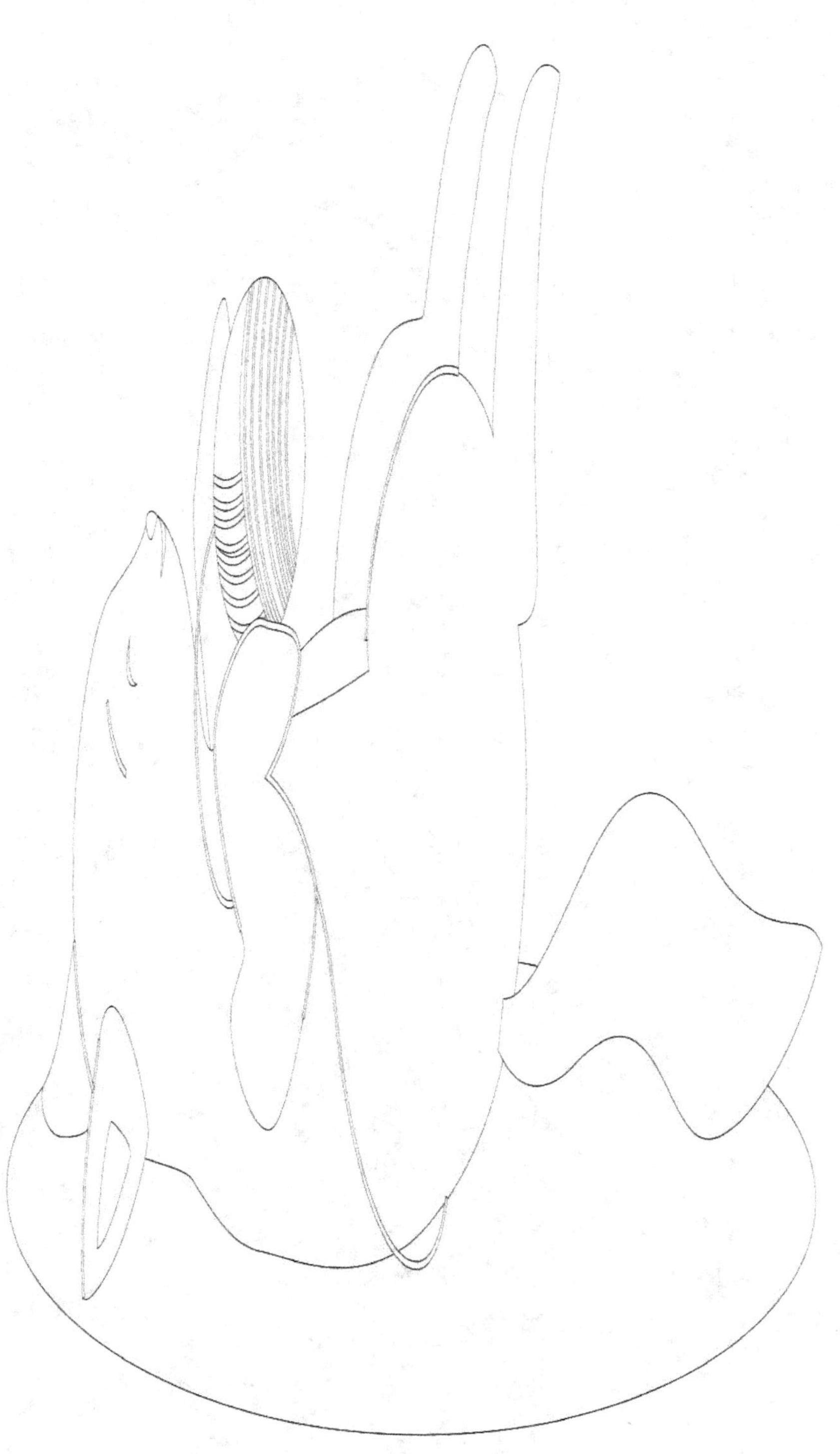

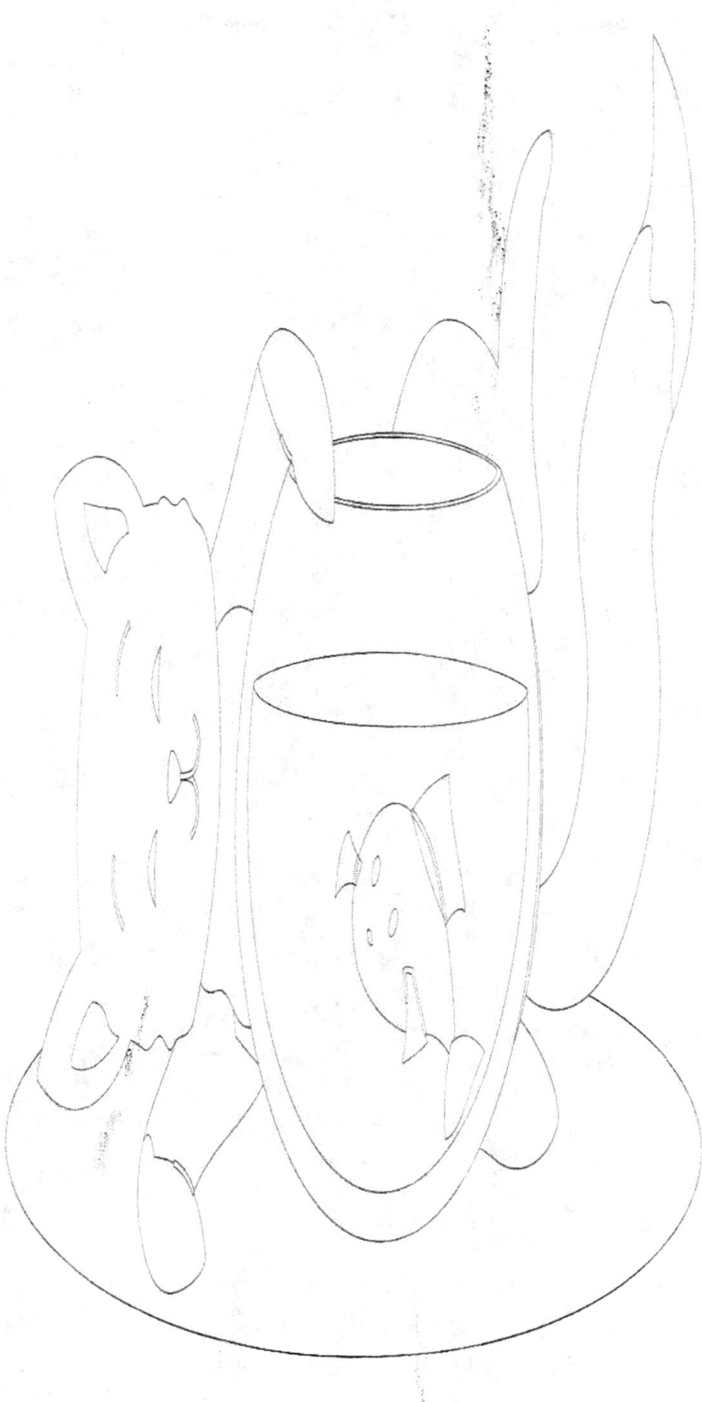

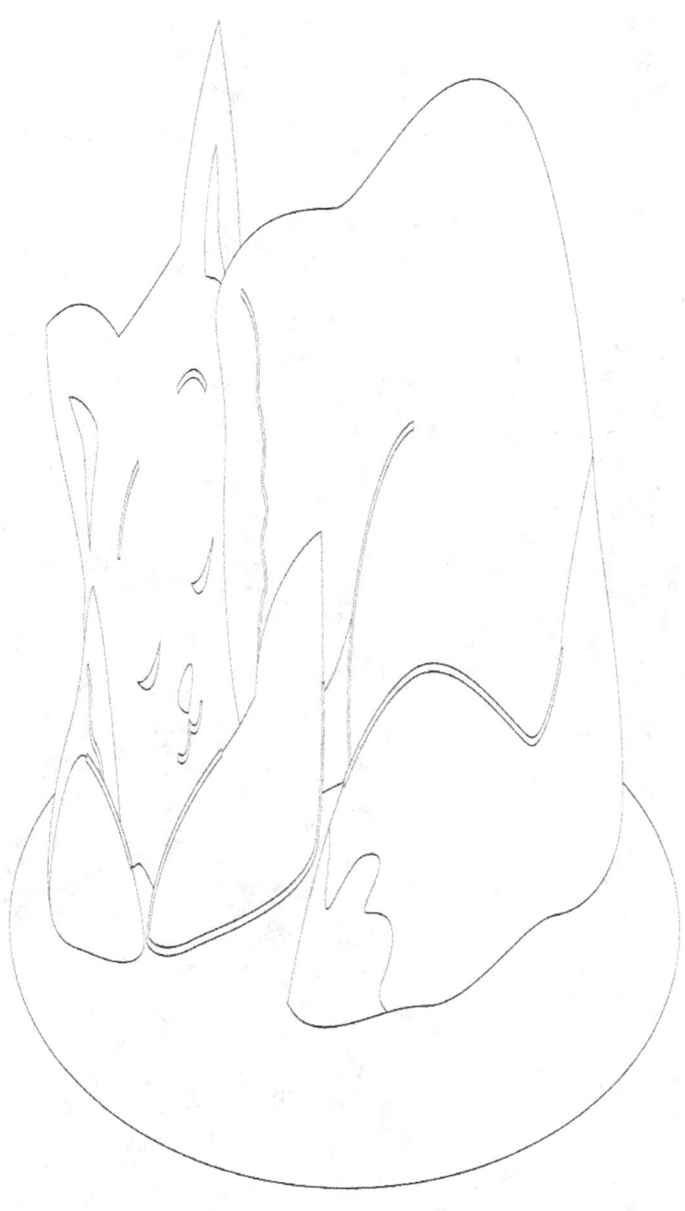

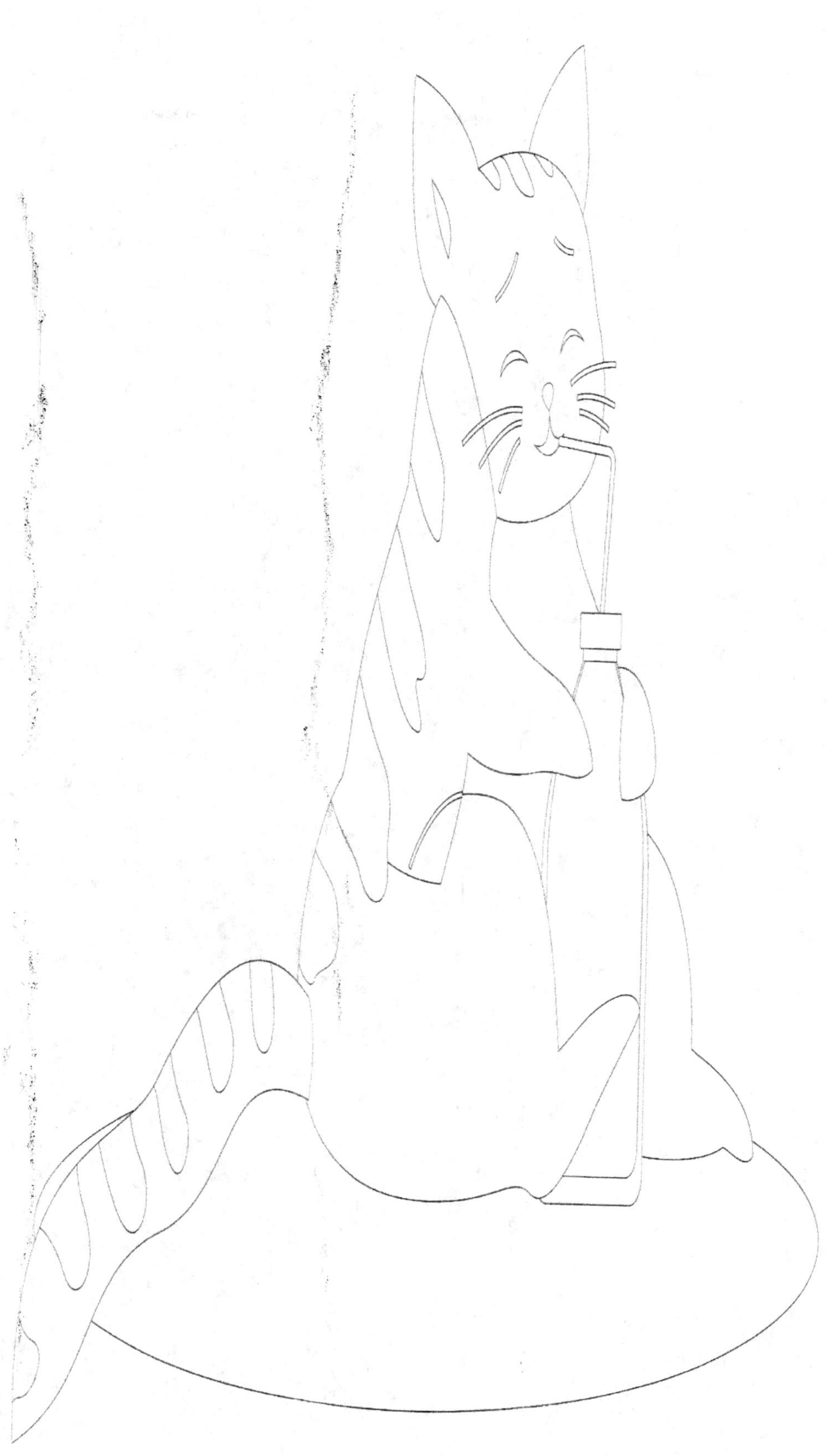

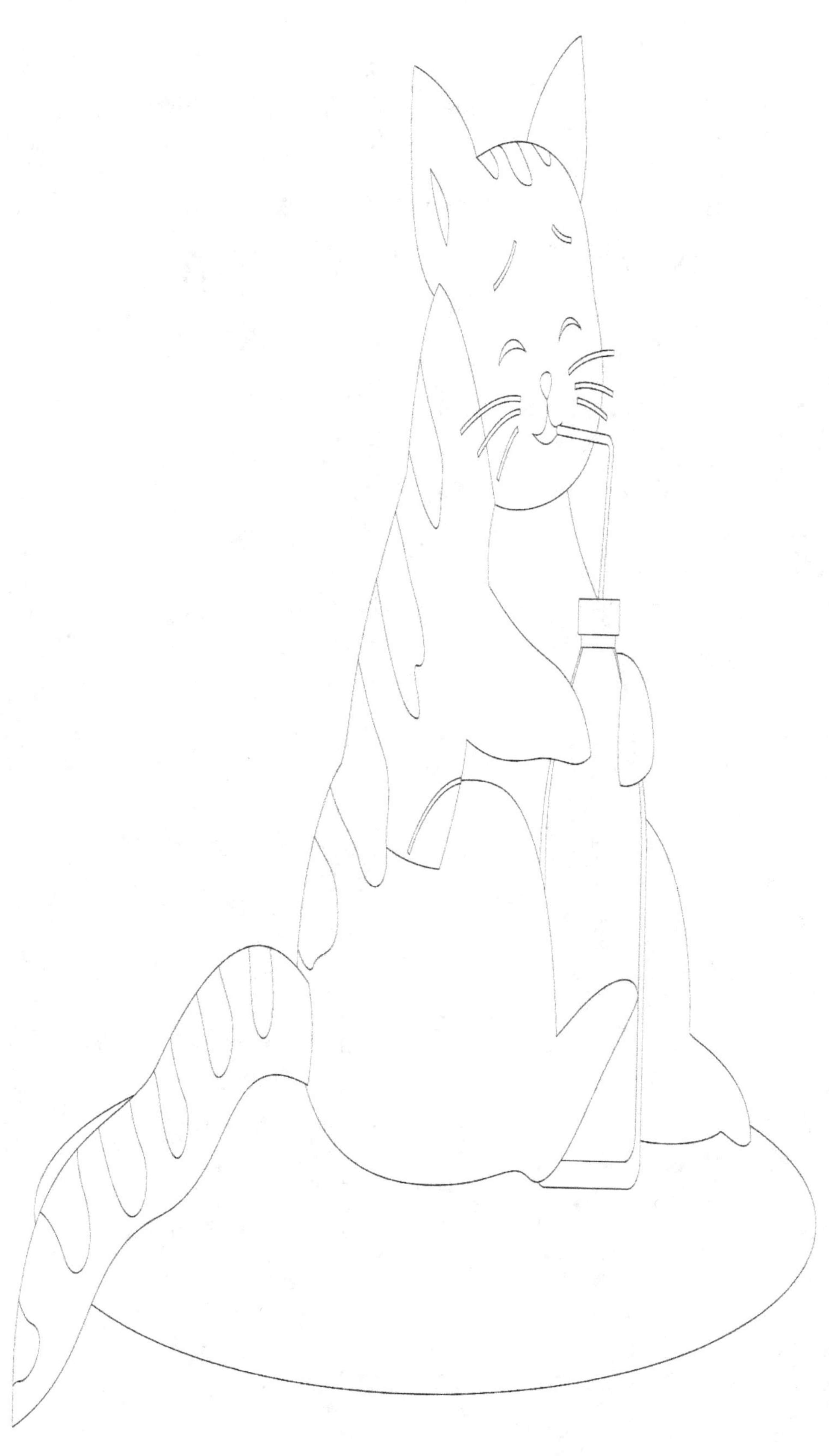

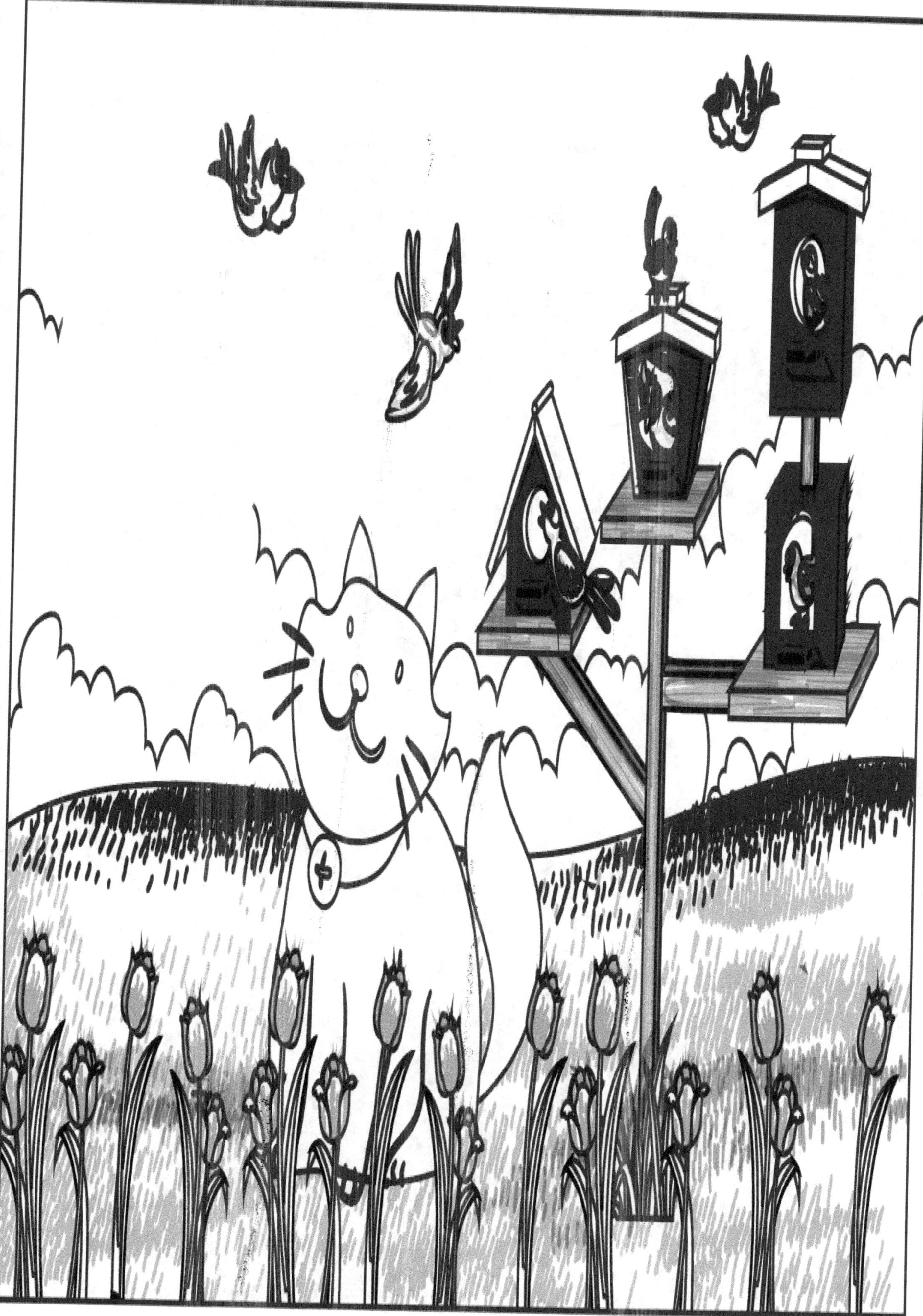

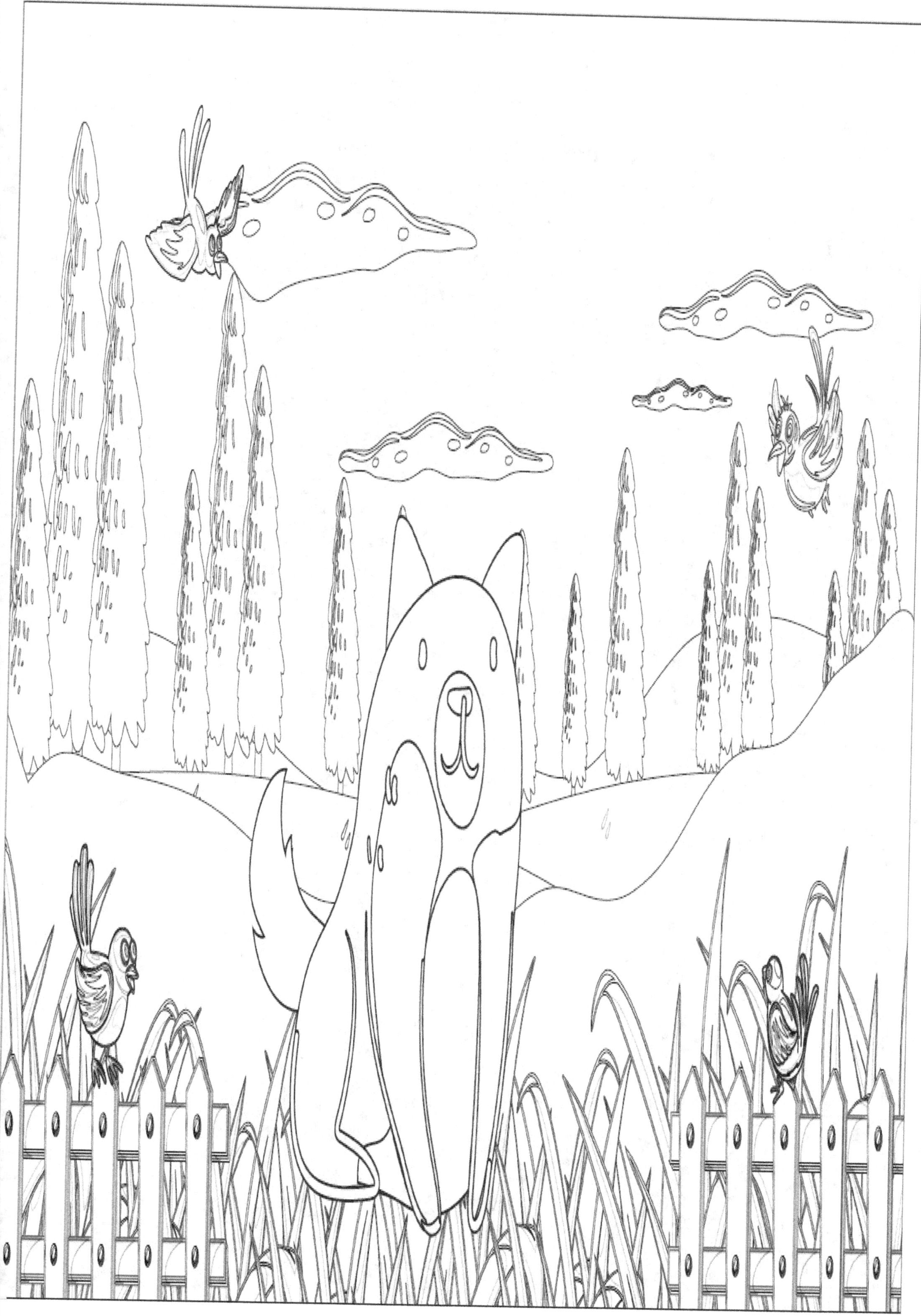

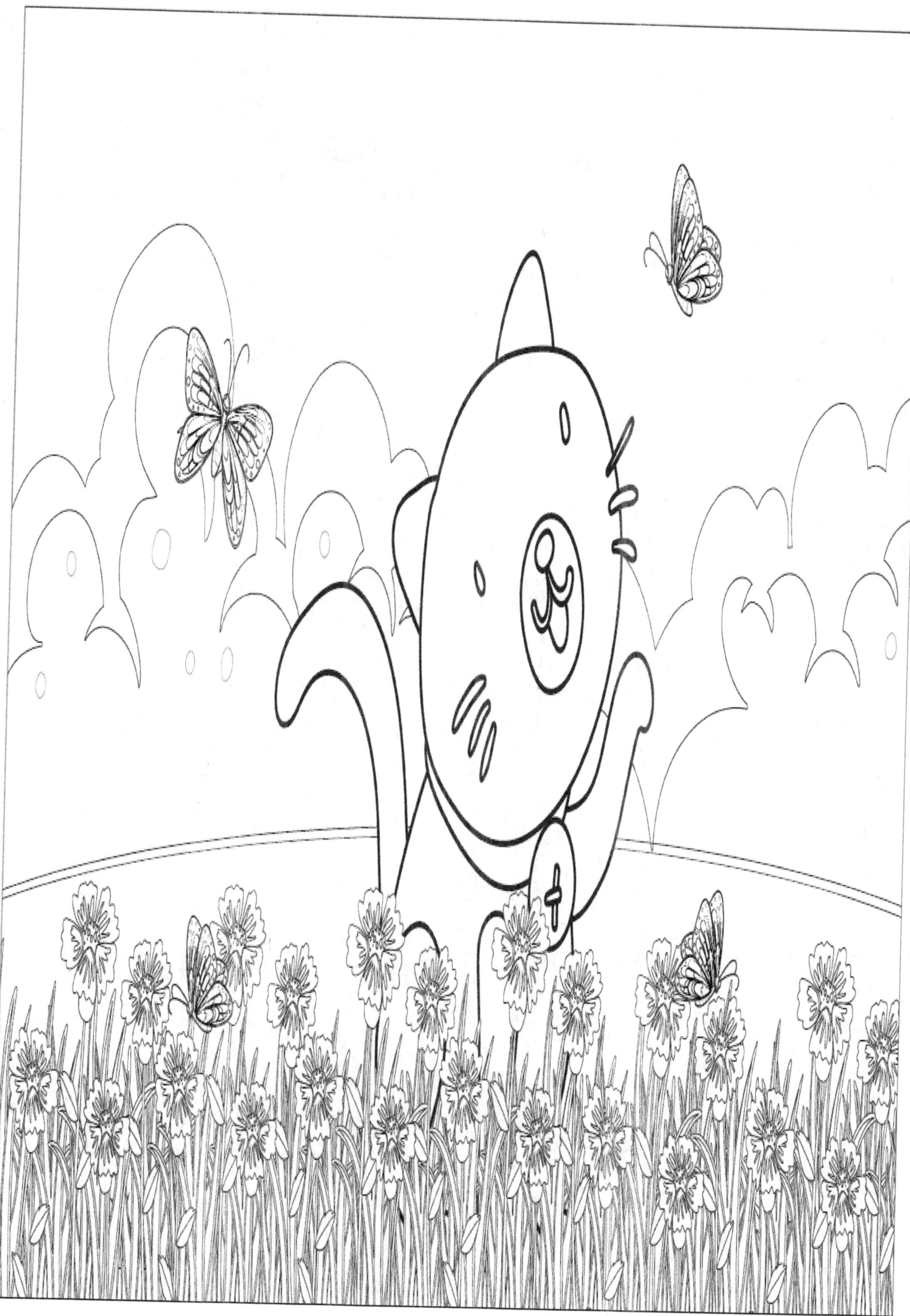

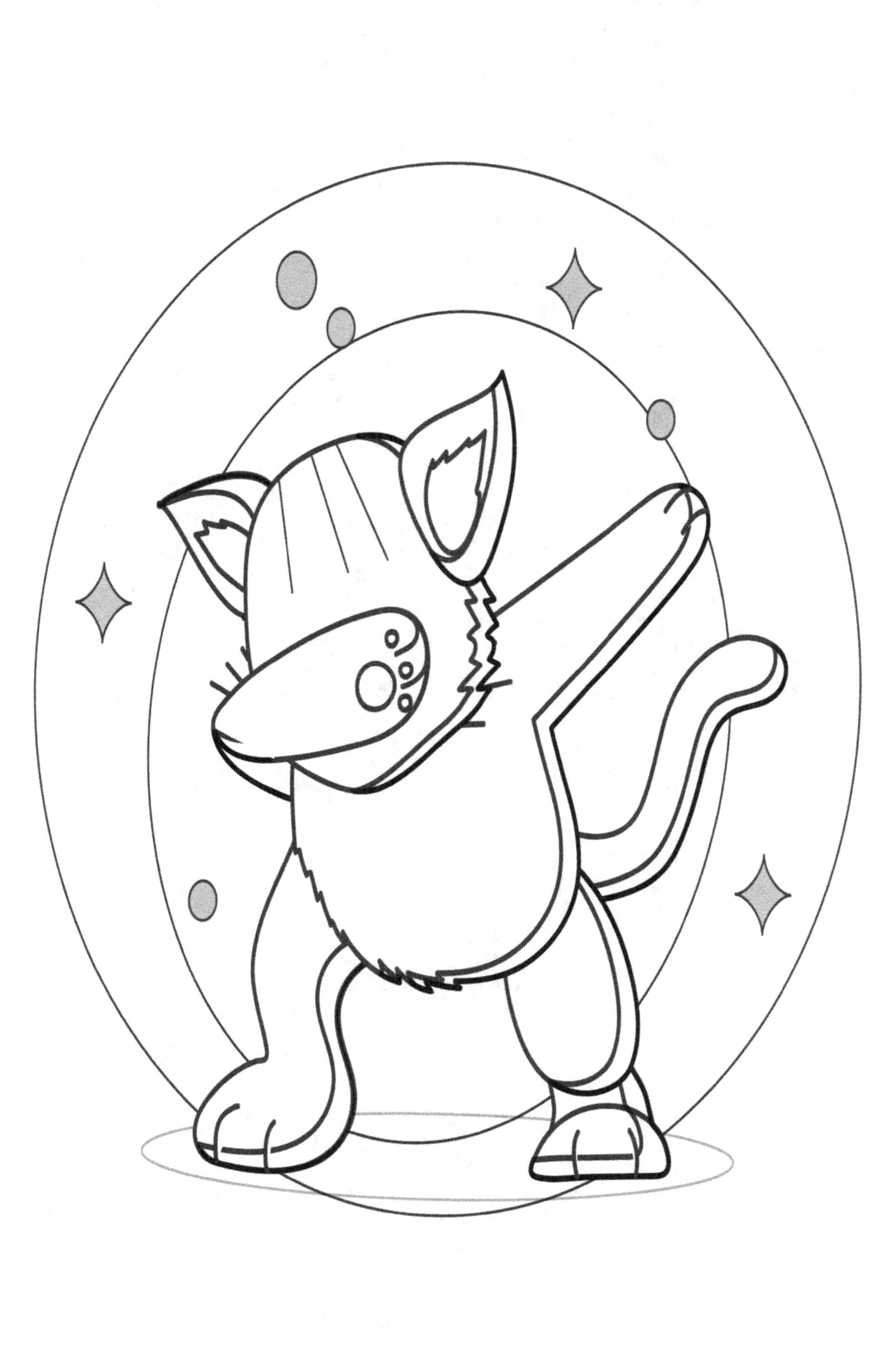

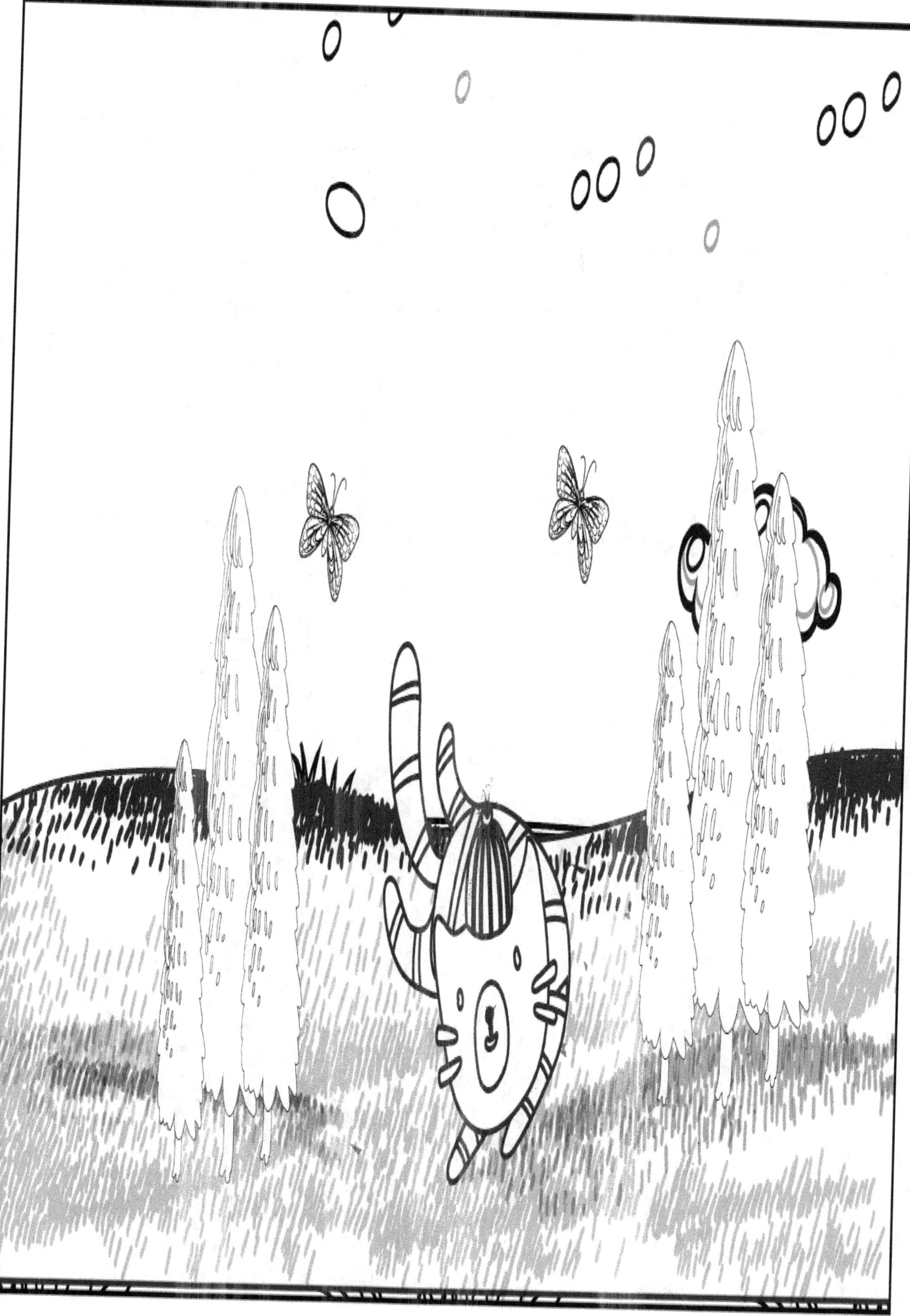

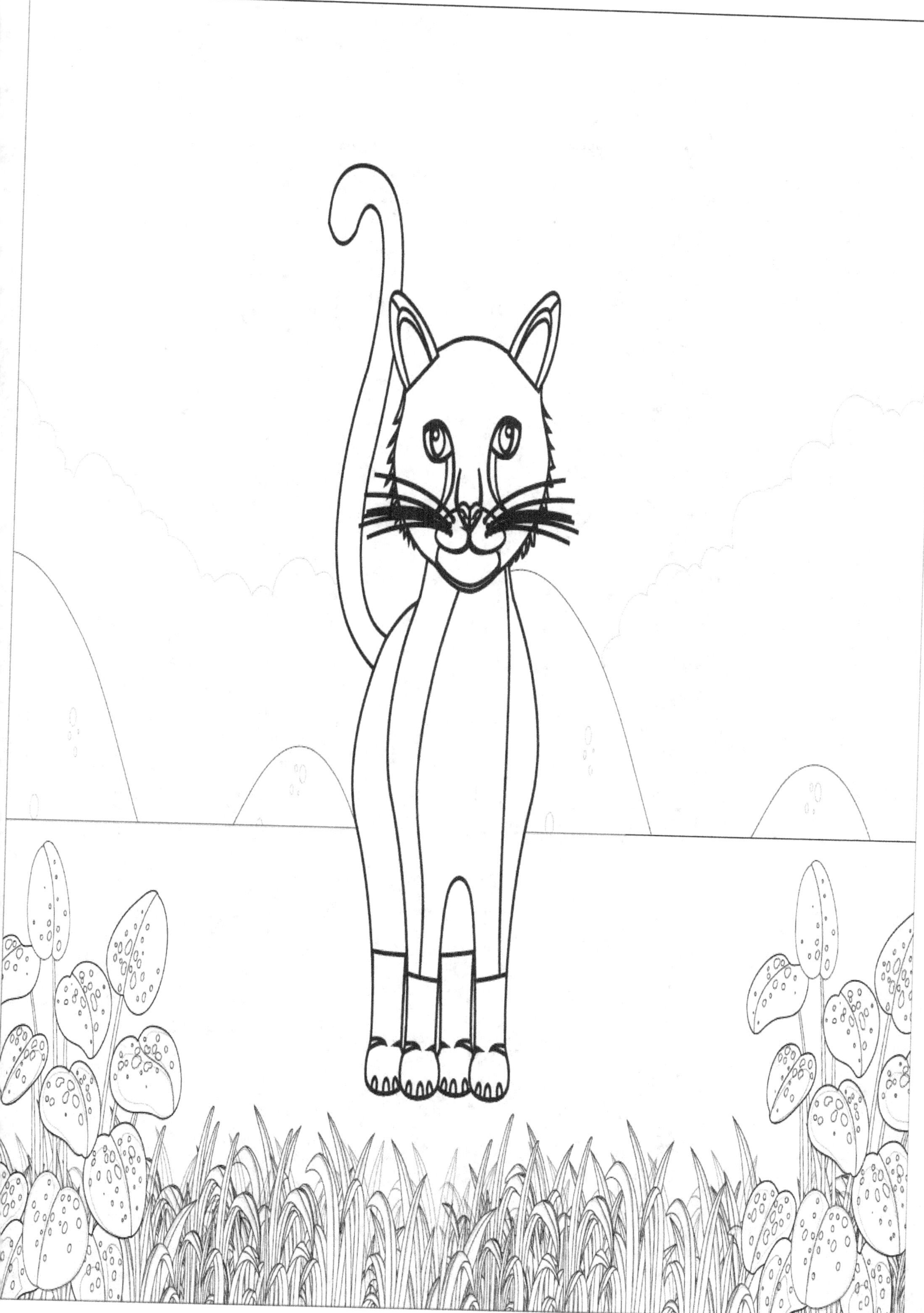

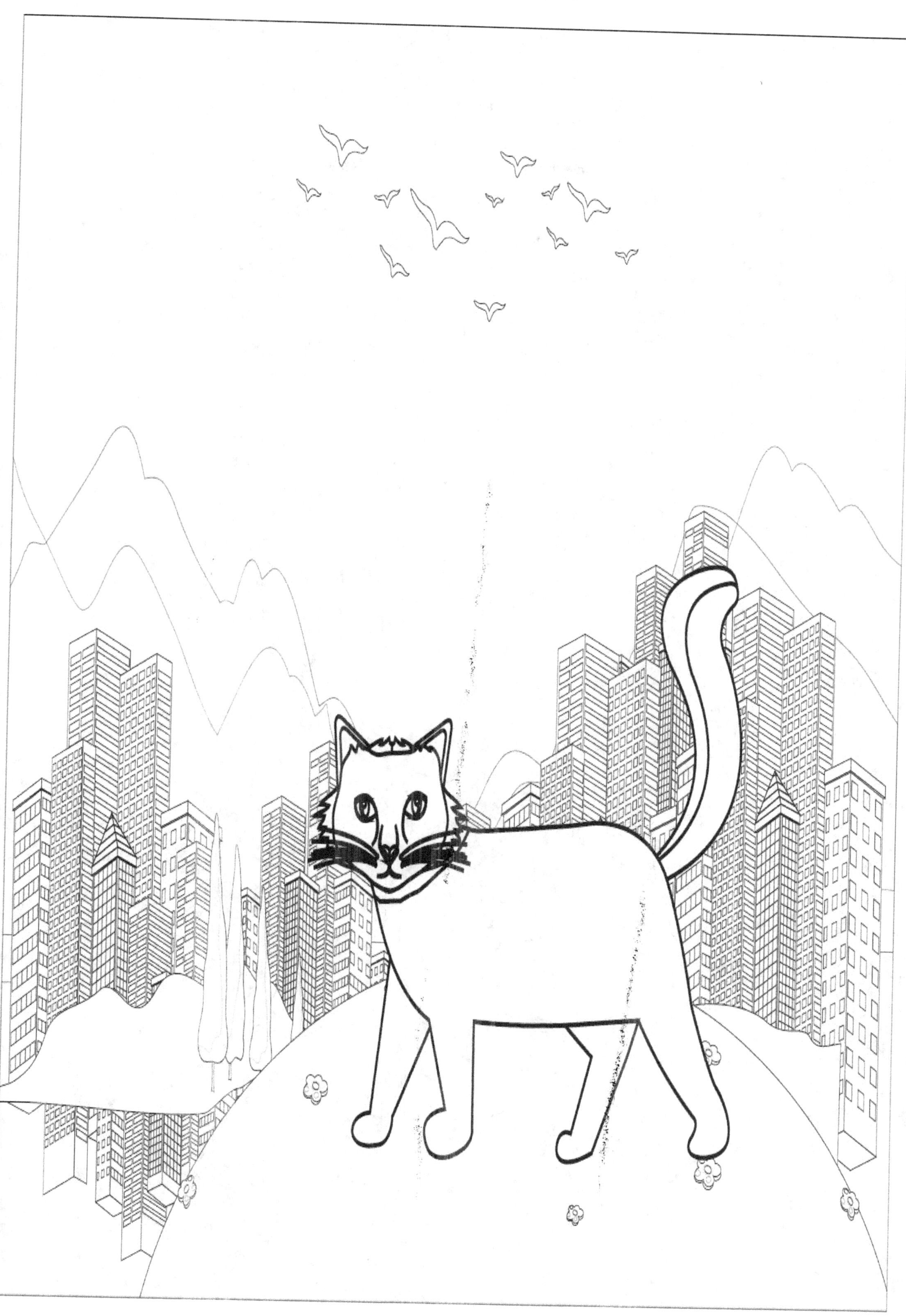

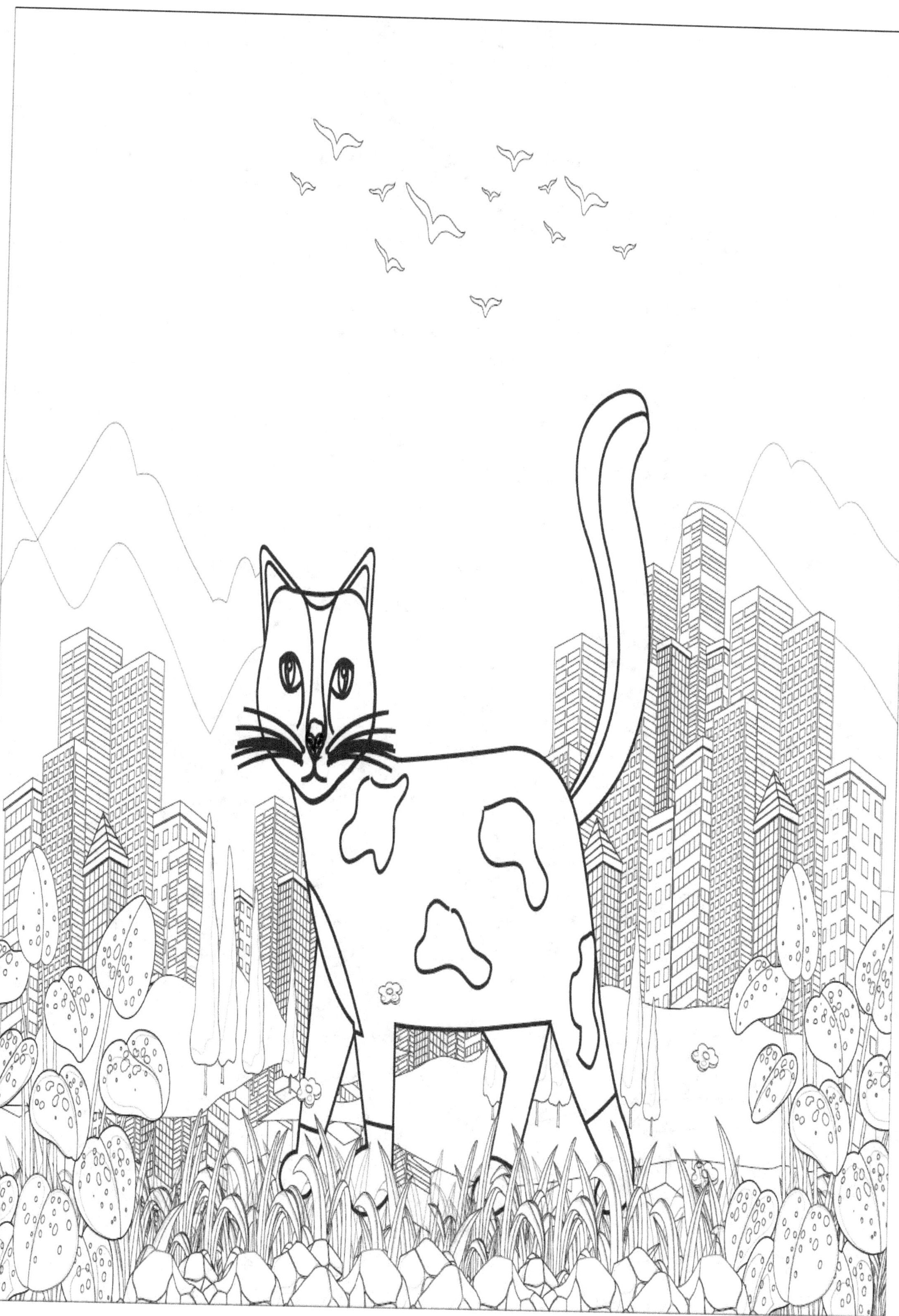

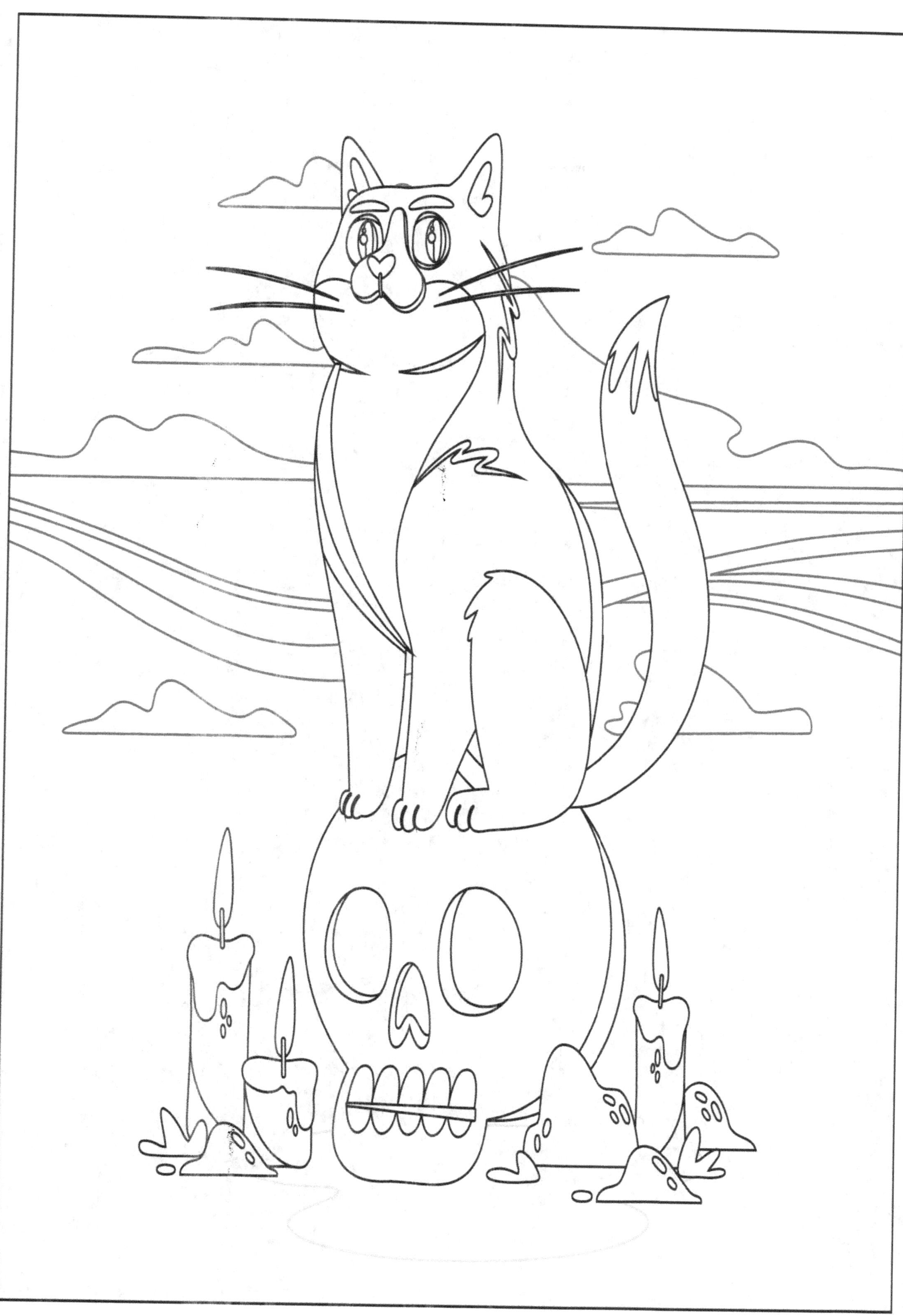

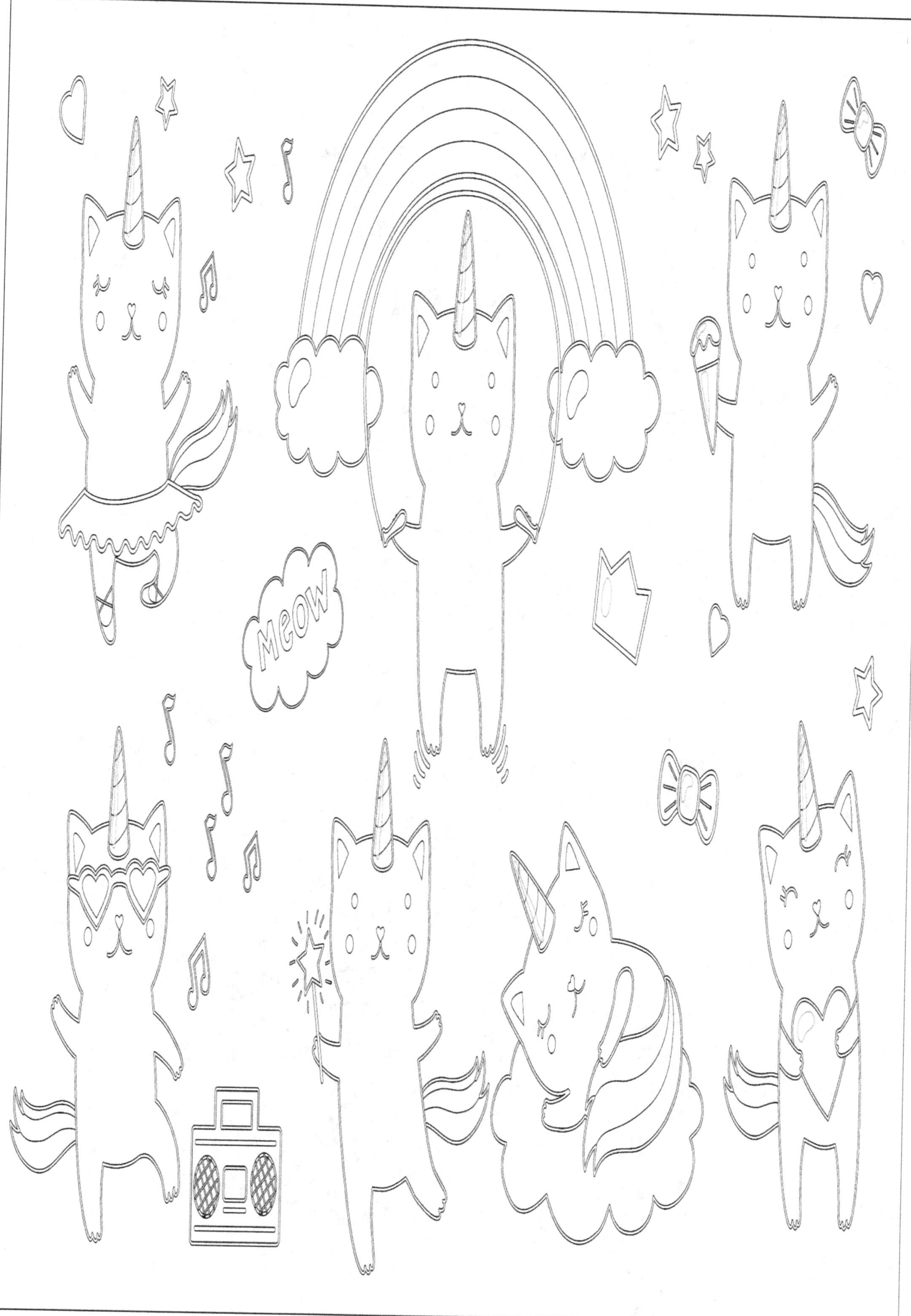

Meow

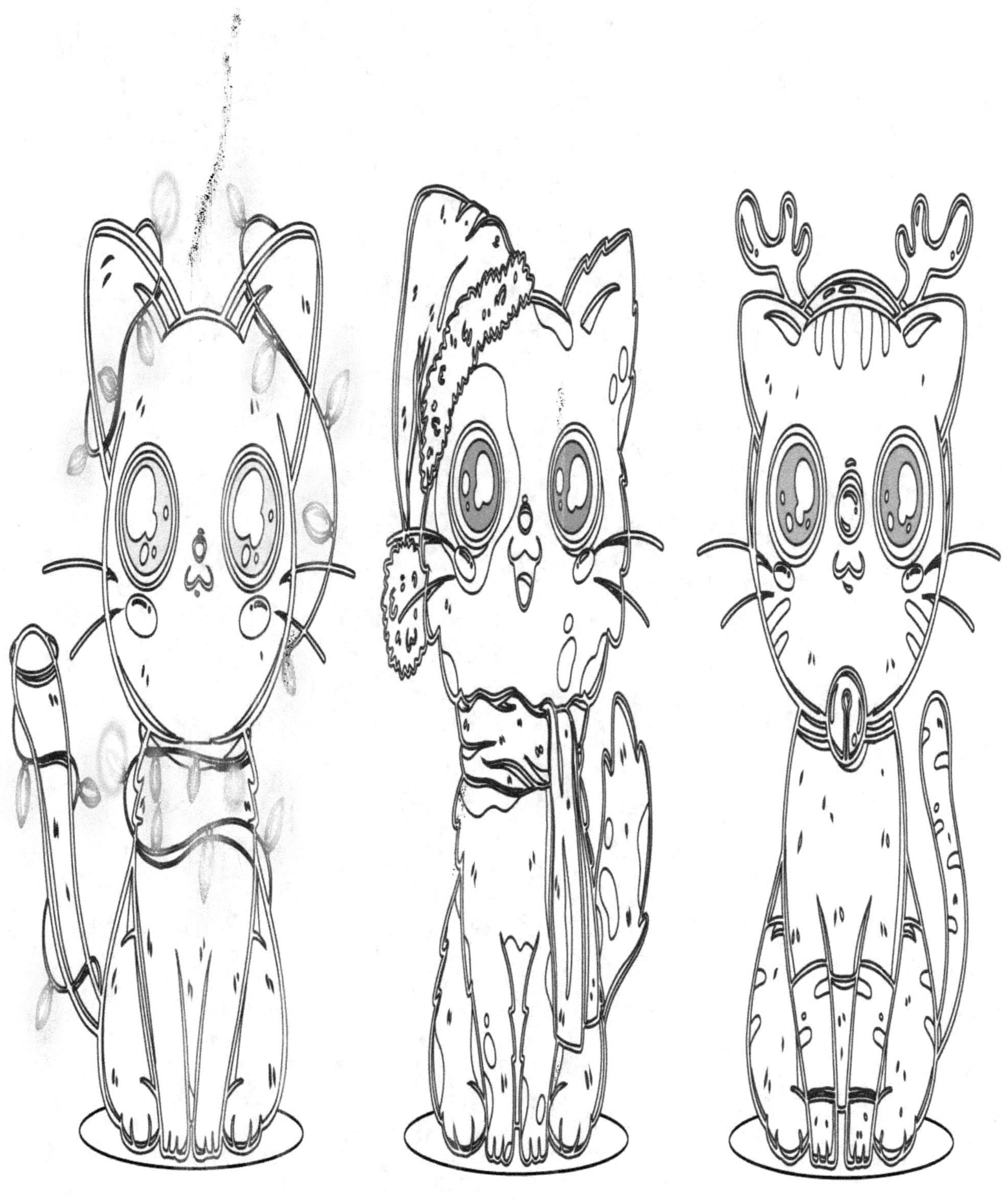

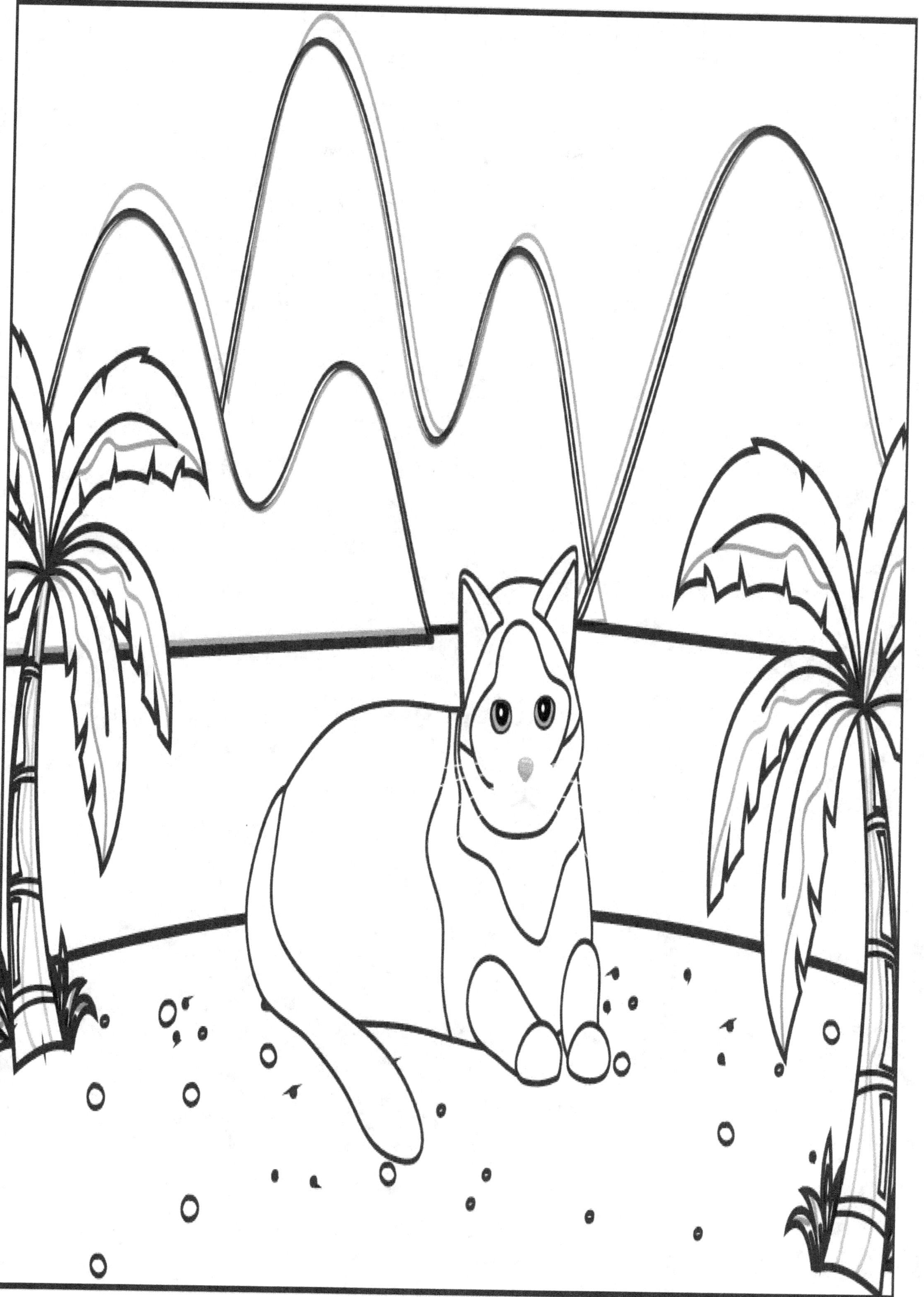

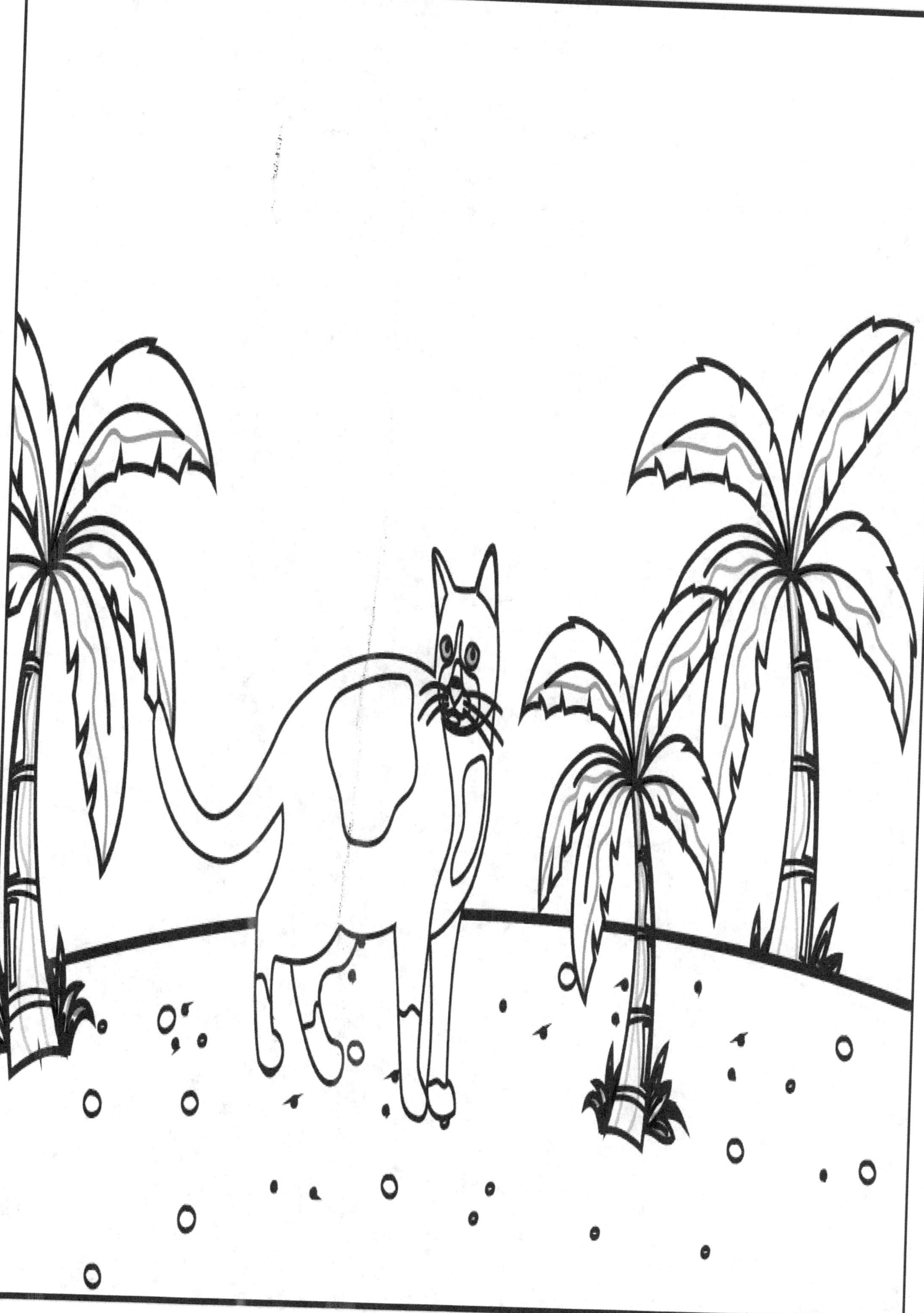